this Notebook
Belong to :

....

....

Made in the USA
Monee, IL
11 March 2021

62520850R00069